Wonders

FLORIDA

Reading/Writing Companion

McGraw Hill

ABOUT THE COVER

Aquariums

Look! It is a green sea turtle. It gets its name from the green fat under its shell. What makes it green? The green sea plants the turtle eats! To find food, the sea turtle uses its strong flippers to swim. The sea turtle uses its sharp jaws to tear the plants it eats.

Some green sea turtles live at aquariums. You can find many aquariums in Florida. Aquariums are places that help to rescue and protect many animals and plants. These living things all live in or around water. You can see dolphins and penguins. You can see corals and many kinds of colorful fish. Sometimes they see you, too!

mheducation.com/prek-12

McGraw Hill

Send all inquiries to:
McGraw Hill
1325 Avenue of the Americas
New York, NY 10019

ISBN: 978-0-07-700910-6
MHID: 0-07-700910-X

Printed in the United States of America.

5 6 7 8 9 10 11 SWI 26 25 24 23 22 B

Welcome to FLORIDA WONDERS!

We are so excited about how much you will learn and grow this year! We're here to help you set goals for your learning.

You will explore new ideas by reading different texts.

Each week, we will set goals on the My Goals page. Here is an example:

I can read and understand texts.

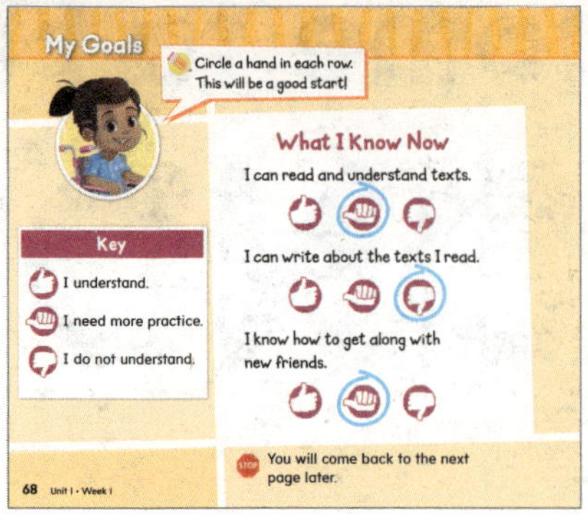

My Goals

Circle a hand in each row. This will be a good start!

Key

I understand.

I need more practice.

I do not understand.

What I Know Now

I can read and understand texts.

I can write about the texts I read.

I know how to get along with new friends.

You will come back to the next page later.

68 Unit 1 • Week 1

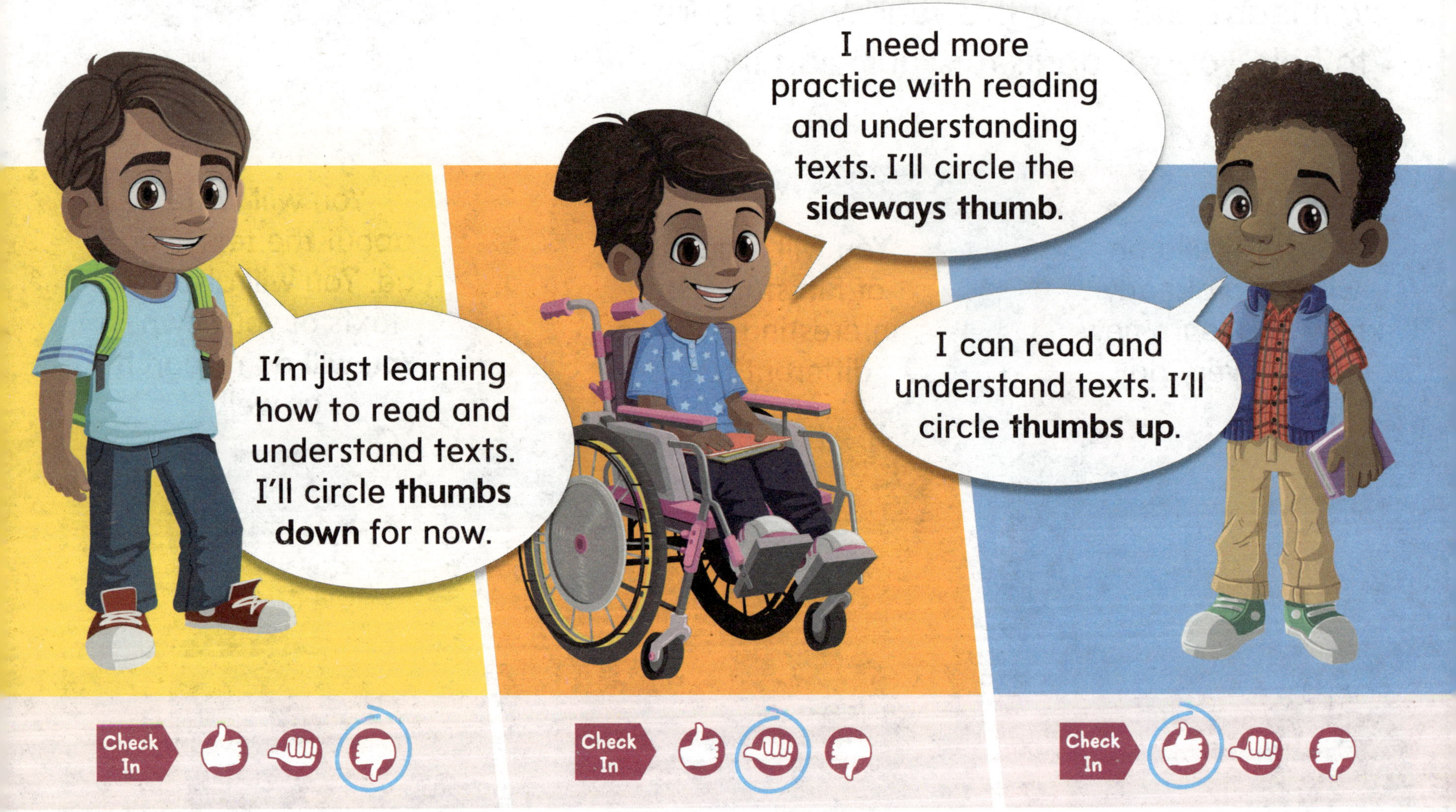

As you read and write, you will learn skills and strategies to help you reach your goals.

You will think about your learning and sometimes circle a hand to show your progress.

Here are some questions you can ask yourself.

- Did I understand the task?
- Was it easy?
- Was it hard?
- What made it hard?

If you need more help, you can choose what to do.

- Talk to a friend or teacher.
- Use an Anchor Chart.
- Choose a center activity.

At the end of each week, you will complete a fun task to show what you have learned.

Then you will return to your My Goals page and think about your learning.

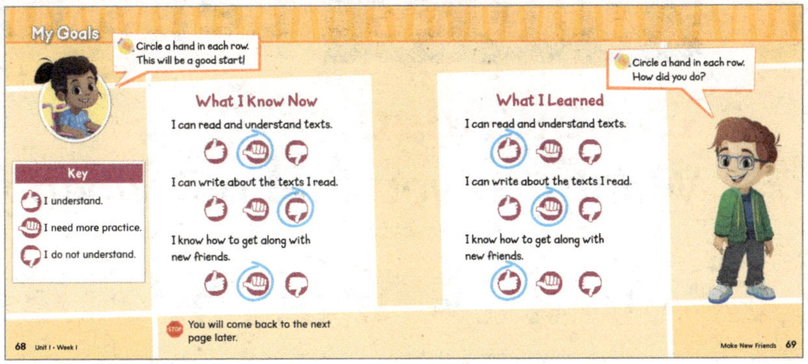
My Goals

Circle a hand in each row. This will be a good start!

Key

I understand.

I need more practice.

I do not understand.

What I Know Now	What I Learned
I can read and understand texts.	I can read and understand texts.
I can write about the texts I read.	I can write about the texts I read.
I know how to get along with new friends.	I know how to get along with new friends.

Circle a hand in each row. How did you do?

You will come back to the next page later.

68 Unit 1 • Week 1

Make New Friends 69

Unit 2 Let's Explore

The Big Idea

Week 1 • Tools We Use

SCIENCE

Digital Tools *Find this eBook and other resources at:* my.mheducation.com

Week 2 • Shapes All Around Us

Week 3 • World of Bugs

Extended Writing

Nonfiction

Connect and Reflect

Judith Cool/Shutterstock

Unit 2

Let's Explore

Talk about what the children are exploring. Speak in a loud, clear voice. Use correct grammar, too.

Circle the things the children are using to explore.

The Big Idea

What can you find out when you explore?

Build Knowledge

Essential Question **How do tools help us to explore?**

Build Vocabulary

Talk about tools that help us explore. What are some words that name different tools?

Draw a picture of one of the tools.

My Goals

Circle a hand in each row.
This will be a good start!

Key

I understand.

I need more practice.

I do not understand.

What I Know Now

I can read and understand texts.

I can write about the texts I read.

I know how tools help us explore.

STOP You will come back to the next page later.

Circle a hand in each row.
How did you do?

What I Learned

I can read and understand texts.

I can write about the texts I read.

I know how tools help us explore.

Respond to the Big Book

Retell the text.

Draw an interesting tool from the text.

Text Evidence

Page

Talk about different tools people use.

Draw and **write** about a tool.
Show how people use this tool.

This tool is a

Reread **Big Book**

A nonfiction text can have photos to help you understand information. Photos can give details about the topic.

Listen to the text.

Talk about the topic and details.

Write the topic.

The topic is

____

____

Draw one detail.

Check In

Reread Big Book

Look at pages 10–11.

Talk about something that is alike in both photos. Share something that is different.

Draw what is different.

Look at pages 34–35.

Talk about ways “the hand itself is handiest.”

Draw and **write** your ideas.

The hand is handiest for

Shared Read

Find Text Evidence

Read to find out the tools Pam can see.

Read and point to each word in the sentence.

Pam Can See

Pam can see a  .
pot

Shared Read

Find Text Evidence

Circle things whose names begin with the same sound as **Pam**.

Underline and read the word **a**.

Pam can see a  .

pen

Pam can see a  .

Shared Read

Find Text Evidence

Circle Sam.

Ask questions you have after reading the story. Then retell the story.

Pam can see a  .
pillow

Pam can see Sam!

Look at the photos.
How can tools help us explore?

Circle the tool that the boy uses to explore.

Draw a box around what the tool helps him see better.

Quick Tip

You can use these sentence starters:

The tool the boy uses is a ____.

The boy can see ____.

Talk about how the tool helps the boy to explore.

Draw something you can explore with this tool.

Talk About It

Talk about what the little photo helps you learn.

Find Text Evidence

Ask questions you have before reading the text. Then read to find out what these children can see.

Circle a thing whose name ends with the same sound as **sap**.

We Can See!

Image Source/Vetta/Getty Images

We can see a map.

Mike Booth/Alamy Stock Photo

Shared Read

Find Text Evidence

Underline and read the word **a**.

Circle an animal that is in the water.

We can see a  .

parrot

Jill Stephenson/Alamy Stock Photo

We can see a  .

seal

image100/Punchstock

Shared Read

Find Text Evidence

Circle animals whose names begin with the same sound and letter as **Pam**.

Retell the text. Use the words and photos to help you.

We can see a .

panda

Can the  panda see the  parrot?

(t)Jill Stephenson/Alamy Stock Photo; (c)DLILLC/Corbis/VCG/Getty Images

Tools for Exploring

Step 1 **Talk** about tools that help scientists explore. Choose one to learn about.

Step 2 **Write** a question about how scientists use this tool.

Step 3 **Look** at books or use the Internet.

Step 4 **Draw** what you learned.

Step 5 **Choose** a good way to present your work.

Integrate

Make Connections

Gunter Marx/BI/Alamy Stock Photo

Look at this art. Try to name the tools it is made from.

Compare this art to the tools you read about this week.

Quick Tip

You can use these sentence starters:

This art is made from ___.

The tools we read about are ___.

Show Your Knowledge

Pack a Tool

1. **Think** about the texts you read. What did you learn about how tools help us explore?

2. **Talk** about a place where you want to go. **Draw** one tool that could help you explore that place.

3. **Write** about why you chose this tool. Use a few words that you learned this week.

Build Knowledge

Essential Question What shapes do you see around you?

Build Vocabulary

Talk about different shapes.
What are some words that name different shapes?

Draw a picture of one of the shapes.

Don Farrall/Photodisc/Getty Images

My Goals

Circle a hand in each row.
You will learn a lot this week!

Key

I understand.

I need more practice.

I do not understand.

What I Know Now

I can read and understand texts.

I can write about the texts I read.

I know shapes I see around me.

STOP You will come back to the next page later.

Circle a hand in each row.
You are doing great!

What I Learned

I can read and understand texts.

I can write about the texts I read.

I know shapes I see around me.

Read

Respond to the Big Book

Retell the text.

Draw an interesting fact from the text.

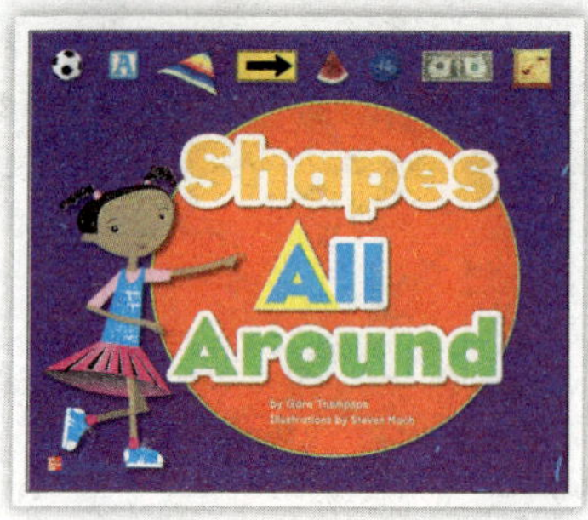

Text Evidence

Page

Talk about shapes you see around you.

Draw one of these shapes.

Write the name of the shape.

The **topic** is what a nonfiction text is mostly about. **Details** help you understand the topic.

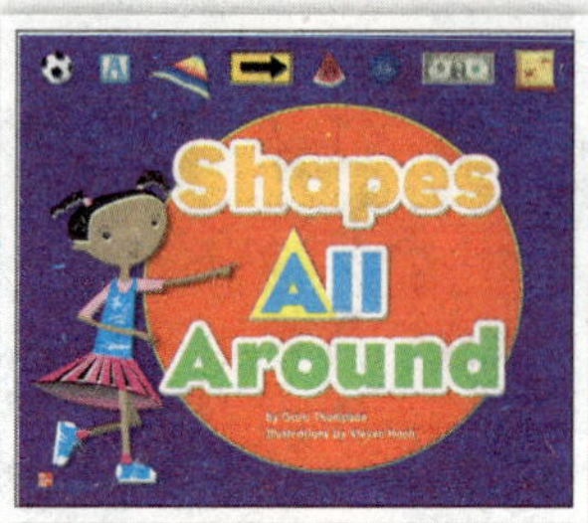

- **Listen** to the text.
- **Talk** about the topic and details.
- **Write** the topic.

The topic is

Draw one detail.

Check In

Reread Big Book

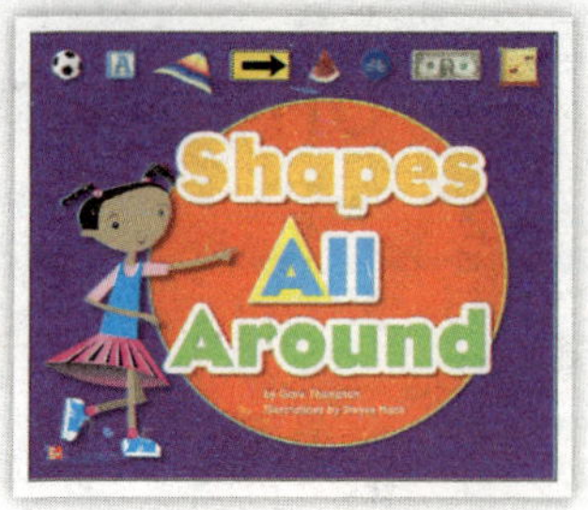

Look at pages 10–11.

Talk about things in the pictures you have seen.

Draw these things.

Look at page 22. What shapes do you see?

Talk about the name of each shape.

Draw and **write** about the shapes.

One shape I see is a

Find Text Evidence

Read to find out about Tam.

Underline and read aloud words that begin with the same sound as **tap.**

We Like Tam!

Tam can see Pam.

Shared Read

Find Text Evidence

Underline words that rhyme on page 48.

Circle what Sam can tap on page 49.

Tam can see Sam.

Sam can tap the  .
bell

Shared Read

Find Text Evidence

Underline and read the word **like**.

Ask questions you may have about the story. Then retell the story.

Tam can tap, tap the  .

bell

We like Tam!

Reread

Paired Selection

Look at the photos. What two groups of shapes do you see?

Talk about how the things in each group are different.

Circle the square shape that is soft.

Draw a box around the circle shape that can bounce.

Quick Tip

You can say:

The shapes on the left are ____.

The shapes on the right are ____.

Write about how something in each group is different in another way.

One square shape is different because

One circle shape is different because

Talk About It

Talk about other things that have the same shape but are different in other ways.

Shared Read

Find Text Evidence

Read to find out what Sam can do.

Underline a word that ends with the same sound as **sat**.

I Like Sam

Sam can pat the cap.

Shared Read

Find Text Evidence

Circle what Sam can pat.

Underline a word that begins with the same sound as **Tam**.

Sam can pat the  ball.

Sam can tap the  .
drum

Shared Read

Find Text Evidence

Circle and read the word **like**.

Retell the story. Use the words and pictures to help you.

Sam can tap the  .
nut

I like Sam!

Shapes Survey

Step 1 **Talk** about the shapes you see in your classroom.

Step 2 **Write** a question about how many of each shape there are.

Step 3 **Look** around your classroom.

Step 4 **Write** how many of each shape you see.

○	□	△	▭

Step 5 **Choose** a good way to present your work.

Integrate

Make Connections

Talk about the shapes you see in this art.

Compare the shapes in this art to the shapes in *Shapes All Around.*

supermimicry/iStock/Getty Images

Quick Tip

You can use these sentence starters:

The shapes in the art are ___.

The shapes in the text are ___.

Design a House

1. **Think** about the texts you read. What did you learn about shapes you see around you?

2. **Pretend** you are a builder. **Design** a house using shapes.

3. **Write** about the shapes you used. Use words that you learned this week.

Build Knowledge

Essential Question What kind of bugs do you know about?

Build Vocabulary

Talk about different kinds of bugs. What are some words that name different kinds of bugs?

Draw a picture of one of the bugs.

PKG Photography/Moment/Getty Images

My Goals

Circle a hand in each row.
There are no wrong answers!

Key

I understand.

I need more practice.

I do not understand.

What I Know Now

I can read and understand texts.

I can write about the texts I read.

I know different kinds of bugs.

STOP You will come back to the next page later.

Circle a hand in each row.
Keep working hard!

What I Learned

I can read and understand texts.

I can write about the texts I read.

I know different kinds of bugs.

Read

Respond to the Big Book

Retell the poem.

Draw an interesting bug from the poem.

Text Evidence

Page

Talk about ways bugs in the poem move.

Draw a bug you have seen.

Write about how it moves.

This bug

Big Book

Words **rhyme** when they sound alike at the end. The words in a poem often rhyme.

Listen for words that rhyme on pages 10-11.

Talk about how these words help you learn about bugs in a fun way.

Write the words that rhyme.

The rhyming words about bugs are

Draw some of the rhyming words you wrote.

Check In

Reread **Big Book**

Listen to and **look** at pages 4-5.

Talk about how the author shows the words *big* and *small*.

Write about why the words are shown in this way.

The words

Listen to and **look** at pages 22–27.

Talk about how the boy feels about scary bugs. How does the author let you know?

Write your ideas.

The author lets me know by

Shared Read

Find Text Evidence

Read to find out about Pat.

Underline a word that ends with the same sound as mat.

Pat

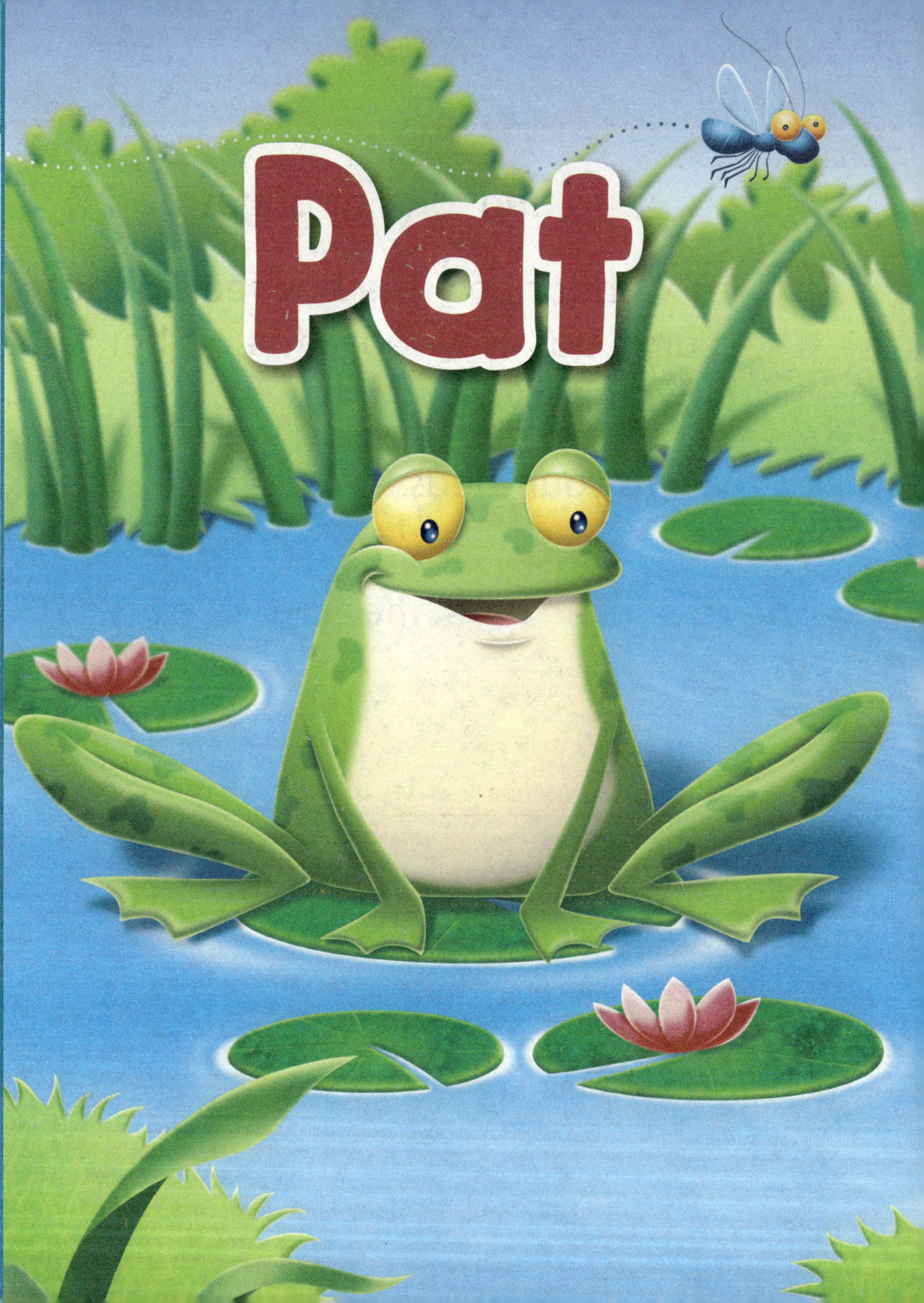

I am Pat.

Shared Read

Find Text Evidence

- **Underline** and read the words *the, see,* and *a.*
- **Circle** what Pat can see.

I am at the  .
rock

I can see a  .
bug

Shared Read

Find Text Evidence

Circle the word that ends with the same sound as **map**.

Retell the story. Use the words and pictures to help you.

I tap the  .

plant

I like the  .

bug

Paired Selection

Look at the photos and captions.
What do they tell about different bugs?

A centipede has many legs.

A grasshopper hops off a leaf.

Circle the caption that tells about the grasshopper.

Draw a box around the caption that tells about the centipede.

Quick Tip

You can use these sentence starters:

The centipede ____.

The grasshopper ____.

Compare the bugs in the photos.

Draw a bug that you learned about.

Write a caption.

Talk About It

How does the author show and tell about bugs?

Tap! Tap! Tap!

Find Text Evidence

Ask questions you may have before reading the text. Then read to find out what the family sees.

Underline words that begin with the same sound as **Tam**.

I am at the  .

lake

Shared Read

Find Text Evidence

Circle what the boy can see on page 85.

Draw a box around the animal whose name begins with the same sound and letter as **and**.

I can see the  .

ant

I can see a  bee .

Martin Ruegner/Photolibrary/Getty Images

Shared Read

Find Text Evidence

Underline and read the words **like** and **We**.

Retell the text. Use the words and photos to help you.

I like to see the  bug!

(t)D. Hurst/Alamy; (b)MIXA/Getty Images

We see it tap, tap, tap!

Bugs

Step 1 **Talk** about different kinds of bugs.
Choose one to learn about.

Step 2 **Write** a question about this bug.

Step 3 **Look** at books or use the Internet.

Step 4 **Draw** what you learned.

Step 5 **Choose** a good way to present your work.

Integrate Make Connections

Talk about the bugs you see. Why does the man wear special clothing?

Compare these bugs to other bugs you read about this week.

Quick Tip

You can use these sentence starters:

These bugs are ___.

Other bugs are ___.

Build a Bug

1. **Think** about the texts you read. What did you learn about different kinds of bugs?

2. **Build** a bug. **Draw** your bug using body parts from the bugs you learned about.

3. **Label** and **describe** your bug. Use words that you learned this week.

Think about what you learned this week.
Turn to page 67.

Writing and Grammar

I wrote a nonfiction text. It has facts about a topic.

Hannah

Nonfiction
My writing has facts about a caterpillar.

Student Model

The Caterpillar

The caterpillar eats many leaves. Then the caterpillar changes into a butterfly!

Genre Study

Talk about what makes Hannah's writing nonfiction.

Ask any questions you have about nonfiction.

Underline one more fact.

Plan

Talk about topics for a nonfiction text. Choose one to write about.

Draw about your topic.

Quick Tip

Think about topics you want to learn more about.

Write your topic.

My topic is

Draw one fact about your topic.

Draft

Read Hannah's draft of her text.

Quick Tip

A **draft** is the first writing we do. We write our first ideas in a draft.

Student Model

The Caterpillar

The caterpillar eats leaves.
Then the caterpillar is a butterfly!

Facts
I wrote a fact about my topic.

Writing Skill
I put spaces between words.

Your Turn

Begin to write your nonfiction text in your writer's notebook. Use your ideas from pages 94–95.

Revise and Edit

Think about how Hannah revised and edited her writing.

Student Model

The Caterpillar

The caterpillar eats ^many leaves.
Then the caterpillar ^changes into a butterfly!

I added a detail to make my writing clearer.

I made sure to use **nouns.**

I used a different **verb.**

Grammar

- A **noun,** or naming word, names a person, place, or thing.
- A **verb,** or action word, tells what someone or something is doing.

Your Turn

Revise and edit your writing.
Be sure to use nouns and verbs.
Use your checklist.

Share and Evaluate

Practice presenting your work with a partner. Take turns.

Present your work. Then use this checklist.

Review Your Work	Yes	No
Writing		
I wrote a nonfiction text.	☐	☐
I added details.	☐	☐
I put spaces between words.	☐	☐
Speaking and Listening		
I spoke in a loud, clear voice.	☐	☐
I asked questions.	☐	☐

Talk with a partner about your writing.

Write about your work.

What did you do well in your writing?

What do you need to work on?

Learn About Tools

Listen to "Look and Learn."

Talk about the tools in the text.

Draw something the children observe with the tools.

Compare the tools you learned about.

Write about how people use the tools.

People use the tools to

Quick Tip

You can say:

The tools in the text are ____.

Other tools are ____.

Observe With Tools

Talk about things that you can observe with a magnifying glass.

What to Do

1. **Look** at the rocks with your eyes.
2. **Look** at the rocks with a magnifying glass.
3. **Draw** what you see.
4. **Write** about what you observe.

You Need

rocks

magnifying glass

What I Observe

I observe

Extend Your Learning

Choose Your Own Book

Minutes I Read

Write the title of the book.

Tell a partner why you want to read it.
Then read the book.

Write your opinion of the book.

Think About Your Learning

Think about what you learned in this unit.

Share one thing you did well.

Write one thing you want to get better at.

My Sound-Spellings

Aa

a
apple

Bb

b
bat

Cc

c ck k
camel

Dd

d
dolphin

Ee

e
egg

Ff

f
fire

Gg

g
guitar

Hh

h_
hippo

Ii

i
insect

Jj

j
jump

Kk

c k ck
koala

Ll

l
lemon

Mm

m
map

Nn

n
nest

Oo

o
octopus

Pp

p
piano

Qq

qu_
queen

Rr

r
rose

Ss

s
sun

Tt

t
turtle

Uu

u
umbrella

Vv

v
volcano

Ww

w_
window

Xx

x
box

Yy

y_
yo-yo

Zz

z
_s
zipper

Credits: (apple) Stockdisc/PunchStock; (bat) Radlund & Associates/Artville/Getty Images; (camel) Photodisc/Getty Images; (dolphin) Arco Images/Petra Wegner/imageBROKER/Alamy; (egg) Pixtal/age fotostock; (fire) Comstock Images/Alamy; (guitar) Jules Frazier/Photodisc Green/Getty Images; (hippo) Michele Burgess/Corbis; (insect) Photodisc/Getty Images; (jump) Rubberball Productions/Getty Images; (koala) Al Franklin/Corbis; (lemon) C Squared Studios/Getty Images; (map) McGraw-Hill Education; (nest) Siede Preis/Photodisc/Getty Images; (octopus) Photographers Choice RF/SuperStock; (piano) Photo Spin/Artville/Alamy Stock Photo; (queen) Joshua Ets-Hokin/Photodisc/Getty Images; (rose) Steve Cole/Photodisc/Getty Images; (sun) 97/E+/Getty Images; (turtle) Ingram Publishing; (umbrella) Stockbyte/Punch-stock/Getty Images; (volcano) Westend61/Getty Images; (window) Photodisc/Getty Images; (box) C Squared Studios/Photodisc/Getty Images; (yo-yo) D. Hurst/Alamy; (zipper) Matthew Cant/ImageState/Alamy.

Handwriting Models

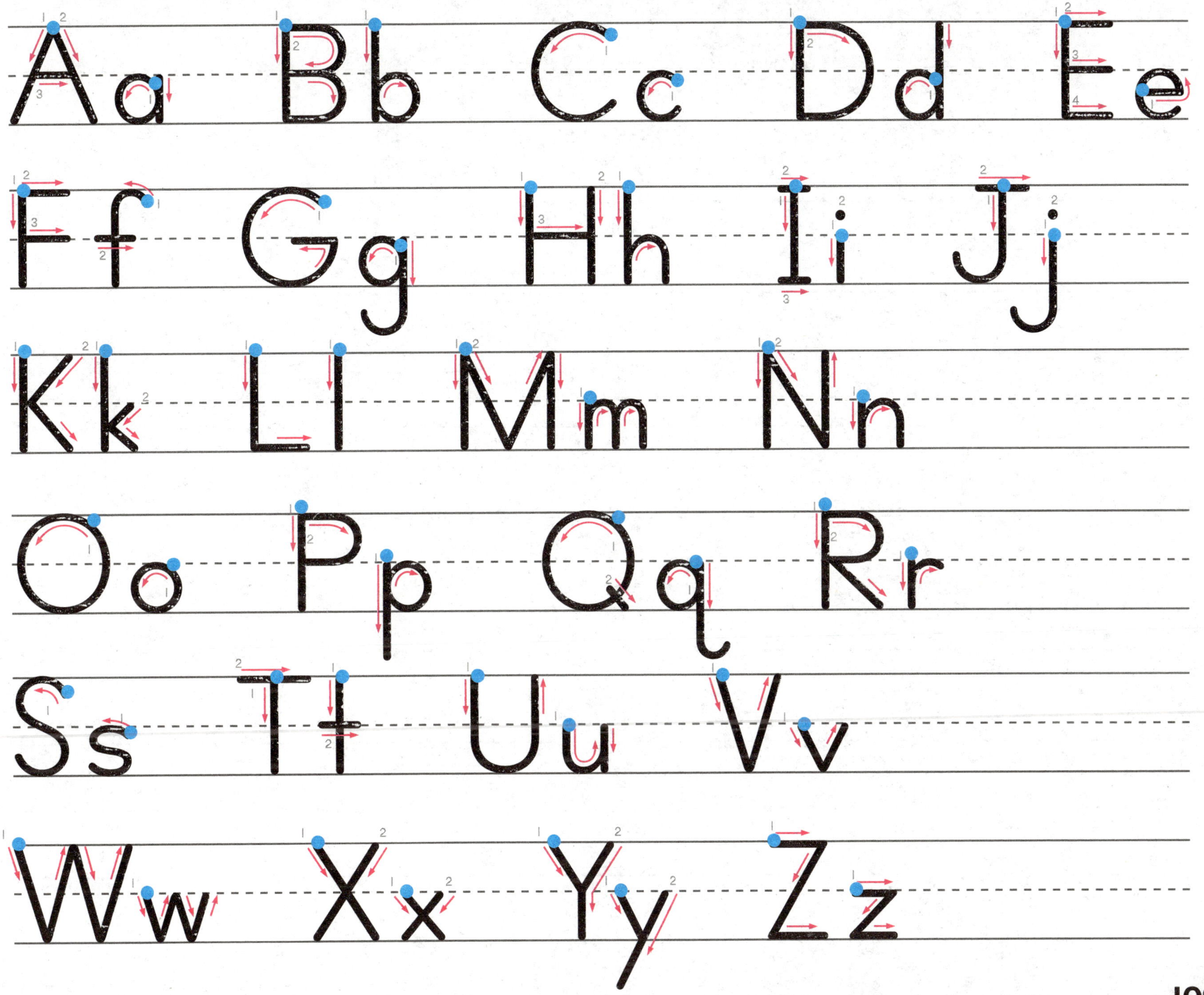